In the United States

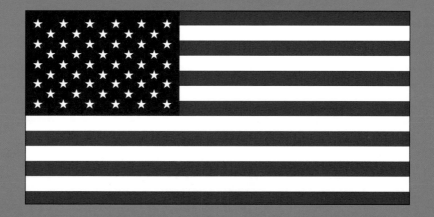

written by **Judy Zocchi** illustrated by **Neale Brodie**

dingles&company New Jersey

For Uncle Bubbie

©2005 by Judith Mazzeo Zocchi

Gumdrop 1038   1-6-2010

First printing

PUBLISHED BY dingles&company
P.O. Box 508 • Sea Girt, New Jersey • 08750
WEBSITE: www.dingles.com • E-MAIL: info@dingles.com

Library of Congress Catalog Card No.: 2004096608
ISBN: 1-59646-085-7

Printed in the United States of America

ART DIRECTION & DESIGN BY Barbie Lambert
EDITED BY Andrea Curley
RESEARCH AND ADDITIONAL COPY WRITTEN BY Robert Neal Kanner
EDUCATIONAL CONSULTANT Bridget Riley Turnbach
PRE-PRESS BY Pixel Graphics

The Global Adventures series takes children on an around-the-world exploration of a variety of fascinating countries. The series examines each country's history and physical features as well as its most popular customs, activities, and foods.

Global Adventures

Judy Zocchi

is the author of the Global Adventures, Holiday Happenings, Click & Squeak's Computer Basics, and Paulie and Sasha series. She is a writer and lyricist who holds a bachelor's degree in fine arts/theater from Mount Saint Mary's College and a master's degree in educational theater from New York University. She lives in Manasquan, New Jersey, with her husband, David.

Neale Brodie

is a freelance illustrator who lives in Brighton, England, with his wife and young daughter. He is a self-taught artist, having received no formal education in illustration. As well as illustrating a number of children's books, he has worked as an animator in the computer games industry.

In the United States REDWOODS are the tallest trees.

Redwood trees are found near the coasts of California and Oregon and are the world's tallest living things. They grow as tall as 360 feet and live for 600 to 1,200 years.

ENGLISH
is the
spoken word.

The United States does not have an official language, although English is used for all government business.

U.S. DOLLARS are what people spend.

The United States dollar is the official currency of the United States. One U.S. dollar equals 100 cents.

The BALD EAGLE is the national bird.

The bald eagle is unique to North America and can be seen in every state in the U.S. except Hawaii. As a symbol of unlimited freedom, the bald eagle became the national emblem when the Great Seal of the United States was adopted in 1782.

In the United States the TELEPHONE was invented.

The first telephone system was installed in New Haven, Connecticut, in 1878, two years after Alexander Graham Bell invented the telephone. Operators sat at a switchboard, answered incoming calls, and connected them manually to the people being called.

LITTLE LEAGUE BASEBALL
is fun to play.

This international youth organization is made up of individual local baseball leagues from all 50 states and more than 70 countries. All of the leagues use the same baseball rules and regulations. The top 16 leagues from around the world compete in an annual Little League World Series.

Alligators live in the EVERGLADES.

The Everglades is a long, wide, grassy marsh at the southern tip of Florida. It has a large variety of plants and animals, including alligators, which float by the river's edge to quickly grab their prey!

Families have cookouts on FATHER'S DAY.

Father's Day is celebrated on the third Sunday of June. It is a day for the family to show appreciation for their father. In 1910 Sonora Smart Dodd of Spokane, Washington, first thought of the holiday because her father single-handedly raised her and her five siblings.

In the United States the world's first SKYSCRAPER was built.

The first skyscrapers were built in Chicago, Illinois, and New York City in the 1880s. Today New York City has the most skyscrapers of any city in the world, with Chicago having the second most.

Names of
BROADWAY SHOWS
light up the street.

Originally named for Broadway, a street in New York City where some theaters are located, the term "Broadway" now refers to any theater that shows professional, large-scale musicals and plays.

MOUNT RUSHMORE
is a giant sculpture.

The faces of four American presidents are carved into the side of a granite mountain in the Black Hills of South Dakota. It took sculptor Gutzon Borglum and his team fourteen years to complete. Millions of people visit this national memorial every year.

MAINE LOBSTERS
are delicious to eat.

Lobsters are found in abundance in the icy waters off the coast of Maine. Maine lobsters are the most popular variety because their flesh is very sweet. Lobsters are usually boiled or broiled.

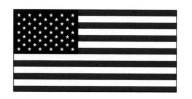

American culture is fun to learn.

REDWOODS

ENGLISH

U.S. DOLLARS

BALD EAGLE

TELEPHONE

LITTLE LEAGUE BASEBALL

EVERGLADES

FATHER'S DAY

SKYSCRAPER

BROADWAY SHOWS

MOUNT RUSHMORE

MAINE LOBSTERS

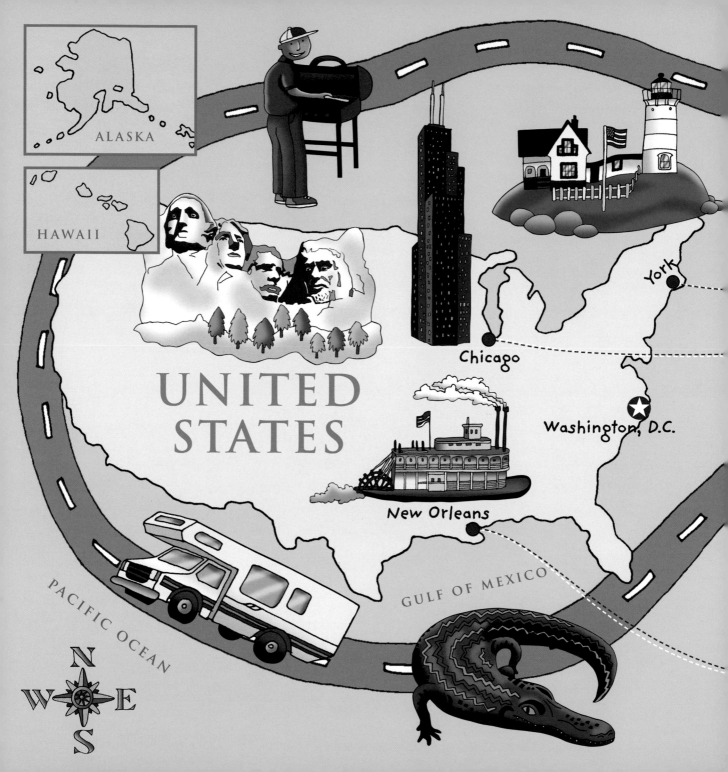

ALASKA

HAWAII

UNITED
STATES

York

Chicago

Washington, D.C.

New Orleans

PACIFIC OCEAN

GULF OF MEXICO

N
W E
S

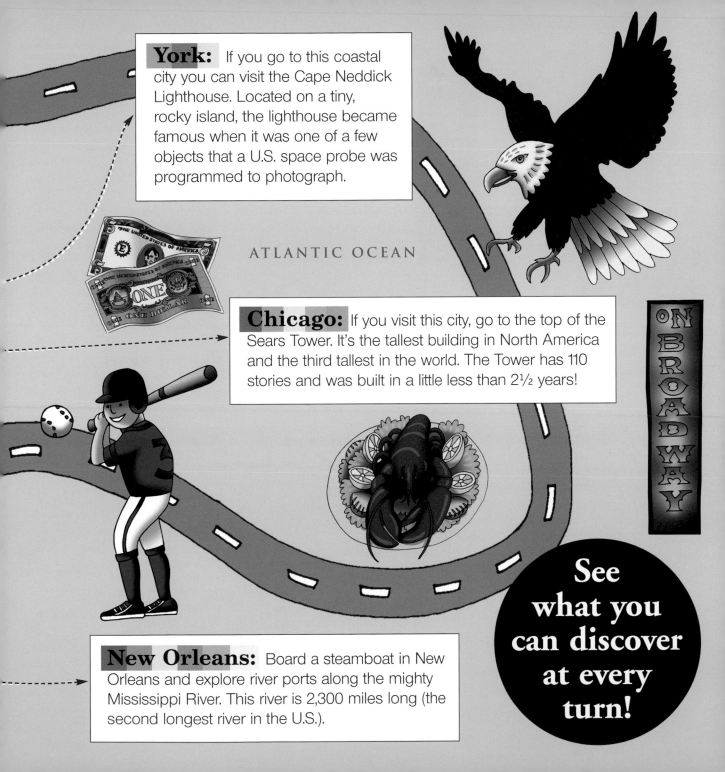

York: If you go to this coastal city you can visit the Cape Neddick Lighthouse. Located on a tiny, rocky island, the lighthouse became famous when it was one of a few objects that a U.S. space probe was programmed to photograph.

ATLANTIC OCEAN

Chicago: If you visit this city, go to the top of the Sears Tower. It's the tallest building in North America and the third tallest in the world. The Tower has 110 stories and was built in a little less than 2½ years!

ON BROADWAY

See what you can discover at every turn!

New Orleans: Board a steamboat in New Orleans and explore river ports along the mighty Mississippi River. This river is 2,300 miles long (the second longest river in the U.S.).

OFFICIAL NAME:
United States of America

CAPITAL:
Washington, D.C.

CURRENCY:
United States dollar

MAJOR LANGUAGE:
English

BORDERS:
Canada, Atlantic Ocean,
Gulf of Mexico, Mexico,
Pacific Ocean

CONTINENT:
North America

ABOUT THE UNITED STATES

Native peoples have lived in the area that became the United States since prehistoric times. During the 1500s people from Great Britain came and founded thirteen colonies on the eastern shores of the region. In 1776 the colonies declared their independence and a war with Britain followed. In 1778 the British surrendered and the colonies, now called states, formed a country called the United States of America. The nation began expanding and new states were added. By the mid 1800s certain states, mainly in the south, disagreed with the national government about how much power each state should have regarding issues such as slavery. In 1861 a civil war began between the Northern and Southern states. The North won the war in 1865, the country was reunited, and slavery was officially abolished throughout the entire country. In the late 19th and early 20th centuries, the United States continued to grow and expand westward. People from many other countries have settled in the United States, hoping to find a better way of life. By the late 20th century the United States became one of the richest and most powerful countries in the world. The United States now has fifty states and governs many territories, including Puerto Rico, American Samoa, and the U.S. Virgin Islands. It is the third largest country in the world.

UNDERSTANDING AND CELEBRATING CULTURAL DIFFERENCES
- What do you have in common with other children from the United States?
- What things do you do differently from other children in the United States?
- What is your favorite new thing you learned about the United States?
- What unique thing about your culture would you like to share with children from other cultures?

TRAVELING THROUGH THE UNITED STATES
- If you traveled from north to south on the parkway through the "Garden State," which state would you be in?
- In which direction would you be traveling if you were going from Seattle, Washington, to Portland, Oregon?
- In which two states would you find Walt Disney World and Disneyland?

TRY SOMETHING NEW...
Plan a cross-country trip! Invite some friends to help. Using a road atlas of the United States, highlight the routes you would take from east to west. What major attractions and points of interest would you want stop and see?